OUTLAWS AND LAWMEN
Crime and Punishment
in the 1800s

DAILY LIFE IN AMERICA IN THE 1800s

OUTLAWS AND LAWMEN
Crime and Punishment in the 1800s

by
Kenneth McIntosh

Mason Crest Publishers

MASON CREST PUBLISHERS INC.
370 Reed Road
Broomall, Pennsylvania 19008
(866)MCP-BOOK (toll free)
www.masoncrest.com

First Printing
9 8 7 6 5 4 3 2 1

Library of Congress Cataloging-in-Publication Data

McIntosh, Kenneth, 1959–
  Outlaws and lawmen : crime and punishment in the 1800s / by Kenneth McIntosh.
— 1st ed.
      p. cm. — (Daily life in America in the 1800s)
  Includes bibliographical references and index.
  ISBN 978-1-4222-1784-9 (hardcover)   ISBN (series) 978-1-4222-1774-0
  ISBN 978-1-4222-1857-0 (pbk.)   ISBN (pbk series) 978-1-4222-1847-1
  1. Outlaws—United States—History—18th century—Juvenile literature. I. Title.
  HV6446.M385 2011
  973.5—dc22
                        2010017918

Produced by Harding House Publishing Service, Inc.
www.hardinghousepages.com
Interior Design by MK Bassett-Harvey.
Cover design by Torque Advertising + Design.
Printed in USA by Bang Printing.

Contents

Introduction

History can too often seem a parade of distant figures whose lives have no connection to our own. It need not be this way, for if we explore the history of the games people play, the food they eat, the ways they transport themselves, how they worship and go to war—activities common to all generations—we close the gap between past and present. Since the 1960s, historians have learned vast amounts about daily life in earlier periods. This superb series brings us the fruits of that research, thereby making meaningful the lives of those who have gone before.

The authors' vivid, fascinating descriptions invite young readers to journey into a past that is simultaneously strange and familiar. The 1800s were different, but, because they experienced the beginnings of the same baffling modernity were are still dealing with today, they are also similar. This was the moment when millennia of agrarian existence gave way to a new urban, industrial era. Many of the things we take for granted, such as speed of transportation and communication, bewildered those who were the first to behold the steam train and the telegraph. Young readers will be interested to learn that growing up then was no less confusing and difficult then than it is now, that people were no more in agreement on matters of religion, marriage, and family then than they are now.

We are still working through the problems of modernity, such as environmental degradation, that people in the nineteenth century experienced for the first time. Because they met the challenges with admirable ingenuity, we can learn much from them. They left behind a treasure trove of alternative living arrangements, cultures, entertainments, technologies, even diets that are even more relevant today. Students cannot help but be intrigued, not just by the technological ingenuity of those times, but by the courage of people who forged new frontiers, experimented with ideas and social arrangements. They will be surprised by the degree to which young people were engaged in the great events of the time, and how women joined men in the great adventures of the day.

When history is viewed, as it is here, from the bottom up, it becomes clear just how much modern America owes to the genius of ordinary people, to the labor of slaves and immigrants, to women as well as men, to both young people and adults. Focused on home and family life, books in this series provide insight into how much of history is made within the intimate spaces of private life rather than in the remote precincts of public power. The 1800s were the era of the self-made man and women, but also of the self-made communities. The past offers us a plethora of heroes and heroines together with examples of extraordinary collective action from the Underground Railway to the creation of the American trade union movement. There is scarcely an immigrant or ethic organization in America today that does not trace its origins to the nineteenth century.

This series is exceptionally well illustrated. Students will be fascinated by the images of both rural and urban life; and they will be able to find people their own age in these marvelous depictions of play as well as work. History is best when it engages our imagination, draws us out of our own time into another era, allowing us to return to the present with new perspectives on ourselves. My first engagement with the history of daily life came in sixth grade when my teacher, Mrs. Polster, had us do special projects on the history of the nearby Erie Canal. For the first time, history became real to me. It has remained my passion and my compass ever since.

The value of this series is that it opens up a dialogue with a past that is by no means dead and gone but lives on in every dimension of our daily lives. When history texts focus exclusively on political events, they invariably produce a sense of distance. This series creates the opposite effect by encouraging students to see themselves in the flow of history. In revealing the degree to which people in the past made their own history, students are encouraged to imagine themselves as being history-makers in their own right. The realization that history is not something apart from ourselves, a parade that passes us by, but rather an ongoing pageant in which we are all participants, is both exhilarating and liberating, one that connects our present not just with the past but also to a future we are responsible for shaping.

—*Dr. John Gillis, Rutgers University Professor of History Emeritus*

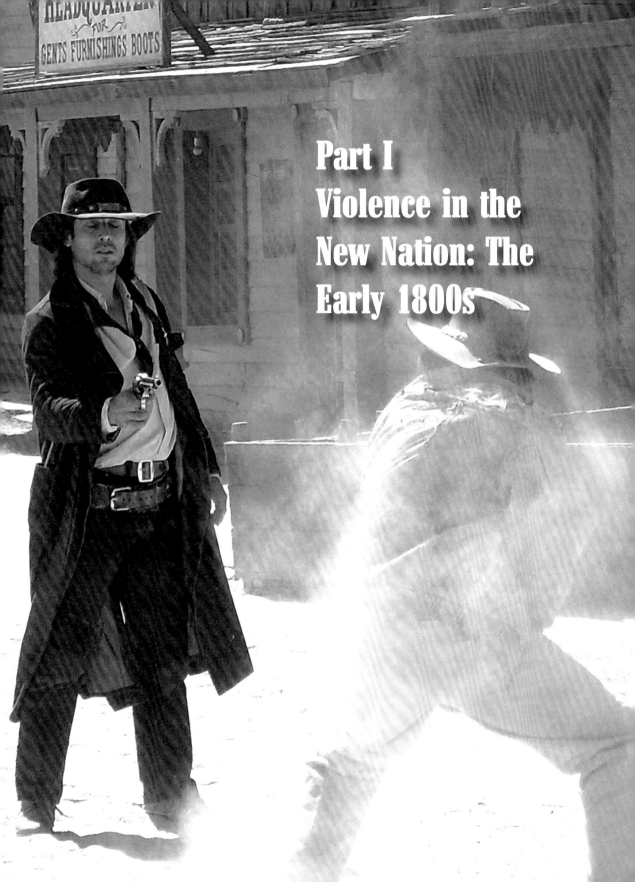

**Part I
Violence in the
New Nation: The
Early 1800s**

1800

1800 The Library of Congress is established.

1801 Thomas Jefferson is elected as the third President of the United States.

1801

1803

1803 Louisiana Purchase—The United States purchases land from France and begins westward exploration.

1820

1820 Missouri Compromise—Agreement passes between pro-slavery and abolitionist groups. It states that all the Louisiana Purchase territory north of the southern boundary of Missouri (except for Missouri) will be free states, and the territory south of that line will be slave.

1823

1823 Monroe Doctrine—States that any efforts made by Europe to colonize or interfere with land owned by the United States will be viewed as aggression and require military intervention.

1823 Texas Rangers form to protect settlers in what is modern-day Texas.

1804

1804 Journey of Lewis and Clark—Lewis and Clark lead a team of explorers westward to the Columbia River in Oregon

1805

1805 Massachusetts State prison opens, and with it the state eliminates use of whipping, branding, and pillory as punishment.

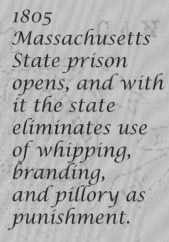

1812

1812 War of 1812—Fought between the United States and the United Kingdom

1825

1825 The Erie Canal is completed—This allows direct transportation between the Great Lakes and the Atlantic Ocean.

1829

1829 Eastern State Penitentiary, the first prison to incorporate solitary confinement, built in Philadelphia, Pennsylvania.

1834

1834 New York and then Pennsylvania become the first two states in the country to ban public executions.

"Put yer hands up!" the man with the badge demands.

The man in black only sneers and gestures toward his gun belt.

"All right then . . . draw!" the lawman retorts.

Wham! Wham! Smoke fills the street, and in a moment, when it clears, one man lies in the dirt.

This is the dramatic image most Americans have in their minds when they think about lawmen and outlaws in the 1800s.

Such men did indeed exist in the Old West, but these characters were only one part of the larger story of crime and punishment in nineteenth-century United States.

Throughout the 1800s, groups of people—slaves of African background, Irish immigrants, First Nations peoples, Spaniards, Mexicans, pro- and anti-slavery activists, gold miners, cattle owners, sheep owners, land owners, and others—struggled to gain control over resources and ensure their survival in the expanding nation. Often, violence was their route to prosperity, and the line between "lawmen" and "outlaws" was drawn more by economic interests than by principles of justice.

INCREDIBLE INDIVIDUAL
Butch Cassidy

Butch Cassidy was a real-life nineteenth-century bad guy. He was born Robert Leroy Parker and grew up on his parents' ranch in Utah. In his early teens, he left home and fell in with Mike Cassidy, a horse thief and cattle rustler. He worked for a little while as a butcher, where he earned the nickname "Butch." He took the name Cassidy in honor of his mentor and friend.

Butch crossed the law for the first time when he journeyed to a clothing shop in another town, only to find the shop closed. He took a pair of jeans anyway, as well as a piece of pie, and left an IOU promising to pay on his next visit. However, the storeowner pressed charges.

Over the next few years, Butch's offenses were far more serious. He held up banks and stole horses. He was arrested, went to prison, was released—and joined a circle of criminals, a gang known as the Wild Bunch. The Wild Bunch was responsible for numerous killings during their robberies.

Reforming Criminal Punishments

"In no country is criminal justice administered with more mildness than in the United States. . . . Americans have almost expunged capital punishment from their codes." In 1835, when visiting Frenchman Alexis de Tocqueville penned these words, the United States was only sixty years old, but it had already made impressive changes in its approaches to crime and punishment.

In the 1700s, authorities punished crimes most often by public ridicule, banishment, or execution. They staged hangings as lavish public ceremonies to impress the public and deter future lawlessness. Then, immediately following the American colonies' declaration of independence from England, the Quakers—who opposed violence in any form—set about reforming criminal laws. The 1776 Pennsylvania constitution included construction of public "houses" to incarcerate criminals, as an alternative to execution.

States designed large penitentiaries (prisons) in the early 1800s to turn criminals into model citizens. The most influential prison was Eastern State Penitentiary, built in Philadelphia, Pennsylvania, in 1829. It featured the "solitary confinement" theory of rehabilitation: as soon as an inmate entered Eastern State, a guard covered his head with a hood so he would not see fellow inmates. Guards did not allow prisoners to socialize, play sports, visit friends from outside, receive letters, or do anything else—except read the Bible and perform physical labor.

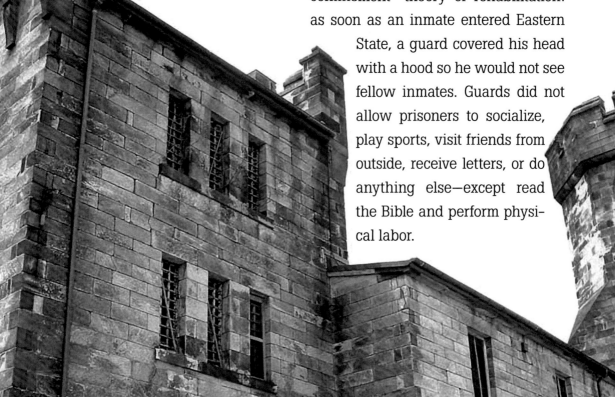

EYEWITNESS ACCOUNT

Two Witnesses—Two Different Views

Alexis de Tocqueville visited Eastern State Penitentiary in 1831. He reported:

Thrown into solitude the prisoner reflects. Placed alone, in view of his crime, he learns to hate it. . . . Can there be a combination more powerful for reformation than that of a prison which hands over the prisoner to all the trials of solitude, leads him through reflection to remorse, through religion to hope?

Eleven years later, Charles Dickens disagreed. In his travel journal in 1842, he wrote:

In its intention I am well convinced that it is kind, humane, and meant for reformation; but I am persuaded that those who designed this system of Prison Discipline, and those benevolent gentleman who carry it into execution, do not know what it is that they are doing. . . . I hold this slow and daily tampering with the mysteries of the brain to be immeasurably worse than any torture of the body.

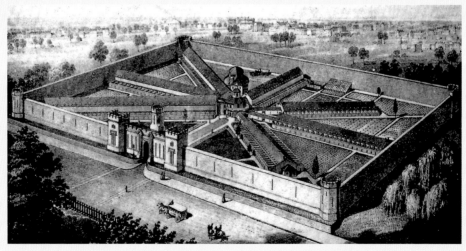

The Eastern State Penitentiary.

Violence Over Immigration Issues: The Gangs of New York

When the Frenchman Alexis de Tocqueville came to the United States in the 1830s, he was impressed by the peaceful state of American society. He could not foresee that waves of violence were about to descend on the United States—first in the East, then later in the West.

From 1845 to 1850, disease wiped out potatoes in Ireland, causing a million deaths from starvation, and sending half a million Irish men, women, and children to the United States. Many Irish died in over-packed vessels known as "coffin ships." When the Irish immigrants arrived, they faced discrimination: they were Catholics, and Protestant Americans did not welcome their faith. Furthermore, the Irish were desperate enough to work for the very lowest wages, and this fueled resentment against the new immigrants, resulting in violence against them.

In 1842, Charles Dickens described the Five Points area of New York, where Irish immigrants lived, as "a world of vice and misery." To survive in these mean streets, Irish immigrants banded together for survival by any means necessary in groups with colorful names like the "Dead Rabbits" or "Bowery Boys." Philip Hone, a New York merchant, wrote in his diary in 1839: "The city is infested by gangs of hardened wretches. . . [They] patrol the streets making the nights hideous and insulting all who are not strong enough to defend themselves." Corrupt politicians, eager for votes and finances, recruited gangs for extortion, running illegal businesses, and violent actions against political opponents. At the same time, more established settlers, ironically calling themselves "Natives," formed their own gangs to fight against the Irish.

Up until 1850, New York City had no official police. When politicians did get around to organizing law enforcement, they actually created two different groups—one called Metropolitans, and the other called Municipals. Citizens recognized the city police by their

The copper badges of the New York City police force may have been why they came to be called "cops."

EXTRA! EXTRA!

DEAD RABBITS' FIGHT WITH THE BOWERY BOYS
New York, July 4 1857.
A song written at Hoboken, by a Saugerties Bard.

They had a dreadful fight, upon last Saturday night,
The papers gave the news accordin';
Guns, pistols, clubs and sticks, hot water and old bricks,
Which drove them on the other side of Jordan.

Like wild dogs they did fight, this Fourth of July night,
Of course they laid their plans accordin';
Some were wounded and some killed, and lots of blood spill'd,
In the fight on the other side of Jordan

The new Police did join the Bowery boys in line,
With orders strict and right accordin';
Bullets, clubs and bricks did fly, and many groan and die,
Hard road to travel over Jordan.

A riot between New York City police and the "Dead Rabbits."

copper badges, which may have been the origin of the term "cop" as slang for police officers. The two rival police forces battled against one another, sometimes freeing criminals imprisoned by the opposing force.

New York Police Chief George W. Matsell, Semi-Annual Report, 1849

Crossings sweepers were among the street children of which Police Chief Matsell complained. He wrote of these children, "Clothed in rags, filthy in the extreme, both in person and in language, it is humiliating to be compelled to recognize them as a part and portion of the human family."

In connection with this report, I deem it my duty, to call the attention of your Honor to a deplorable and growing evil which exists amid this community, and which is spread over the principal business parts of the city. It is an evil and a reproach to our municipality, for which the laws and ordinances afford no adequate remedy.

I allude to the constantly increasing number of vagrants, idle and vicious children of both sexes, who infest our public thoroughfares, hotels, docks, &c.; children who are growing up in ignorance and profligacy, only destined to a life of misery, shame and crime, and ultimately to a felon's doom. Their numbers are almost incredible, and to those whose business and habits do not permit them a searching scrutiny, the degrading and disgusting practices of these almost infants, in the school of vice, prostitution and rowdyism, would certainly be beyond belief. The offspring of always careless, generally intemperate and oftentimes immoral and dishonest parents, they never see the inside of a schoolroom; and so far as our excellent system of public education i[s] concerned, and which may be truly said to be the foundation stone of our free institutions, is to them an entire nullity. Left in many instances to roam day and night wherever their inclination leads them, a large proportion of these juvenile vagrants are in the daily practice of pilfering wherever opportunity offers, and begging when they cannot steal.

INCREDIBLE INDIVIDUAL "Boss" Tweed

William Magear Tweed, known as "Boss" Tweed, excelled at political corruption. He is most famous for his leadership of Tammany Hall, the Democratic Party power block that controlled New York City's politics in the mid-1800s. In the fictional movie, Gangs of New York, Tweed says, "The appearance of law must be

upheld, especially while it's being broken." If he didn't actually say that, he certainly lived by the principle. Controlling the courts, police, and public works, Tweed stole somewhere in the realm of $200 million from New York citizens— that would be 8 billion in today's currency! Tweed was arrested for his crimes and jailed in 1871; he died in prison of pneumonia seven years later.

THE "BRAINS"

EXTRA! EXTRA!

A DEPLORABLE "LODGING HOUSE" FOR IMMIGRANTS IN NEW YORK'S FIVE POINTS

New York Illustrated News, 1859

Down half a dozen ricketty steps, the door was already open to one of the filthiest, blackest holes we had yet seen.

A number of wretched bunks, similar to those on shipboard, only not half as convenient, ranged around an apartment about ten feet square. Nearly every one of the half-dozen beds was occupied by one or more persons. No regard was paid to age or sex; but man, woman, and child were huddled up in one undistinguishable mass. . . . The most fetid odors were emitted, and the floor and the walls were damp with pestiferous exhalations. . . . Not the slightest breath of air reached these infernal holes, which were absolutely stifling with heat.

In response to an inquiry regarding two small children sleeping soundly in one of the hideous beds, the manager replied that their older sister who cared for them was out begging, even at that late hour.

Anglo-American Law Comes to the West– The Texas Rangers

In 1821 Stephen F. Austin arranged for 300 families from the Eastern United States to settle in what was then known as the Spanish Province, what we now call Texas. Two years later, nearly 700 Easterners had moved there. Austin then called these settlers together and asked them to form an armed band for their protection. They called this group, formed in 1823, the Rangers, because their duties required them to "range" over the entire territory.

Early on, the Rangers provided the settlers with protection against Native Americans, who fought to preserve their own homelands threatened by waves of white settlers. Later, in the 1800s, the Rangers enforced the law against cattle rustlers and desperados. This same law enforcement organization—the Texas Rangers—continues to serve today.

One of the Texas Rangers.

Mark Twain's view of Southern justice from "The Adventures of Huckleberry Finn"

In this episode, a lynch mob has gathered, attempting to bring a wealthy citizen, Colonel Sherburn, to justice after he gunned down a drunken man who accosted him. Huck describes the resulting confrontation:

They swarmed up in front of Sherburn's palings as thick as they could jam together, and you couldn't hear yourself think for the noise. . . . Just then Sherburn steps out on to the roof of his little front porch, with a double-barrel gun in his hand, and takes his stand, perfectly ca'm and deliberate, not saying a word. The racket stopped, and the wave sucked back.

Sherburn never said a word—just stood there, looking down. The stillness was awful creepy and uncomfortable. Sherburn run his eye slow along the crowd; and wherever it struck the people tried a little to outgaze him, but they couldn't; they dropped their eyes and looked sneaky. Then pretty soon Sherburn sort of laughed; not the pleasant kind, but the kind that makes you feel like when you are eating bread that's got sand in it.

Then he says, slow and scornful:

"The idea of you lynching anybody! It's amusing. The idea of you thinking you had pluck enough to lynch a man! Because you're brave enough to tar and feather poor friendless cast-out women that come along here, did that make you think you had grit enough to lay your hands on a man? Why, a man's safe in the hands of ten thousand of your kind—as long as it's daytime and you're not behind him. Do I know you? I know you clear through . . . . The average man's a coward. . . . Now leave!"

Snapshot from the Past
Virginia, 1801

Althea Cunningham walked quickly down the cobblestone street past a couple of cart vendors hawking vegetables and fruits, and came to a small brick building with a sign hanging over the door: Debtor's Gaol. She raised and lowered the big brass knocker, and a porter opened the door.

"Yes?"

"I'm here to see my father, James Cunningham, Esquire." She pointed to a basket under her arm, with two loaves of freshly baked bread.

The porter opened the door further, gestured, "This way, ma'am."

A debtors' jail in Virginia, like the one where Althea's father was imprisoned.

The porter took out his keys and unlocked a door behind him, gesturing again for Althea to enter.

"Oh, Father!" Althea ran to her father. He was gaunt, his hair turning prematurely grey, and his clothes fraying, but James Cunningham still had the bearing of a distinguished gentleman as he rose from the wooden bench where he sat.

"Althea! What a delight to see you, dear."

"Mother baked this bread this morning, and— Oh, Father, I cannot believe you are here—I cannot believe the injustice."

He sighed. "It is the law."

"Yes, but you have committed no crime, only fell into financial misfortune."

He shook his hand. "Owing debt I cannot pay—it is not violence, true, but still it is a crime . . . and I must pay the penalty until somehow I make good all my obligations."

"Oh, Father." Althea buried her face in her hands. "How can we earn the money to pay off your debts when you are imprisoned here?"

Part II
Violence and Slavery:
The Civil War Era

1838

1838 Trail of Tears—General Winfield Scott and 7,000 troops force Cherokees to walk from Georgia to a reservation set up for them in Oklahoma (nearly 1,000 miles). Around 4,000 Native Americans die during the journey.

1839

1839 The first camera is patented by Louis Daguerre.

1841

1841 Amistad case comes before the Supreme Court.

1850

1850 The Pinkerton National Detective Agency founded–Pinkerton detectives track hundreds of criminals and bring them to justice.

1854

1854 Kansas-Nebraska Act—States that each new state entering the country will decide for themselves whether or not to allow slavery. This goes directly against the terms agreed upon in the Missouri Compromise of 1820.

1859

1859 John Brown's Rebellion—John Brown leads a revolt and takes over the federal arsenal at Harper's Ferry, Virginia. However, he is soon forced to surrender by U.S. marines, and then is hung for his crimes.

1844

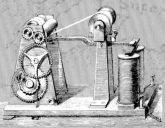

1844 First public telegraph line in the world is opened—between Baltimore and Washington.

1846

1846 Michigan becomes the first state to abolish the death penalty for all crimes except treason.

1848

1848 Seneca Falls Convention—Feminist convention held for women's suffrage and equal legal rights.

1848(-58) California Gold Rush—Over 300,000 people flock to California in search of gold.

1861

1861(-65) Civil War —Fought between the Union and Confederate states.

1862

1862 Emancipation Proclamation—Lincoln states that all slaves in Union states are to be freed.

1865

1865 Thirteenth Amendment to the United States Constitution—Officially abolishes slavery across the country.

1865 President Abraham Lincoln is assassinated on April 15.

Before the Civil War, more than four million slaves suffered from cruel labor, brutal punishments, and loss of their human rights. At the same time, conflict over this unjust practice pitted faction against faction in America.

The *Amistad* Case

In 1839 the Schooner *Amistad* drifted onto the Long Island coast, with two Cuban slave-owners and fifty-three slaves, who had over-thrown their white captors at sea, aboard. This incident raised a series of legal questions: what (if any) crimes had been committed? Who now owned the ship's cargo (includ-ing the slaves)?

The *Amistad* was the scene of a revolt by African captives being transported to Cuba. The schooner had been built in the United States, but a Spaniard living in Cuba owned it. The Africans who took control of the ship were captured off the coast of Long Island by the USS *Washington* of the United States Revenue Cutter Service. The *Amistad* (a Spanish word that means "friendship") became a symbol in the movement to abolish slavery.

A series of trials followed, moving up through the court system. In the meantime, abolitionists (people opposed to the practice of slavery) championed the slaves' cause. In 1841, the case came before the Supreme Court, where former President John Quincy Adams argued in the slaves' defense. The Supreme Court ruled that the *Amistad*'s African passengers were entitled to their freedom.

After the trial, the freed Africans and abolitionists worked together raising money and eventually paid for a ship that carried the freed men, women, and children back to Africa. By affirming the slaves' rights to liberate themselves, the case set a precedent against the practice of slavery.

Kansas Territory and John Brown: The War Before the Civil War

While politicians and activists in the East debated slavery, settlers headed west seeking new lands to settle, bringing with them the issues of the East. The Kansas-Nebraska Act stated that settlers of those territories would decide by popular vote whether or not to allow slavery, but bloody fights broke out between pro- and anti-slavery factions. Battles over slavery caused the Kansas Territory to be known as "Bleeding Kansas."

John Brown became the leader of anti-slavery settlers during the Bleeding Kansas battles. Brown didn't care for the patient and peaceful way most abolitionists worked against slavery.

He said, "These men are all talk. What we need is action—action!"

In 1859 Brown and his followers did something that shocked the nation: they attacked the federal armory at Harpers Ferry, Virginia, hoping to capture guns and ammunition to begin a war for slaves' liberation. Local citizens and the U.S. Marines fought the raiders; half of them were killed, and Brown was captured. Authorities tried Brown for treason, found him guilty, and hanged him.

Brown's bloody campaign was over, but he lived on in poems, songs, and letters—regarded as either a saint or the worst kind of villain.

An artist's interpretation of John Brown as the central symbol of the violence in Bleeding Kansas.

EYEWITNESS ACCOUNT

John Brown's Raid

Alexander Boteler, who was with the civilians fighting against the raiders, describes an attempt at gaining a truce with Brown's forces:

It was thought proper . . . to send Brown a summons to surrender, and a respectable farmer of the neighborhood, Mr. Samuel S——— was selected to make the demand, a duty which he undertook very willingly, although it was not unattended with danger. . . . Tying a white handkerchief to the ferrule of a faded umbrella, he went forth upon his mission.

Marching up to the door of the engine house, he called out in stentorian tones, "Who commands this fortification?"

"Captain Brown, of Kansas," was the answer, from within the building.

"Well, Captain Brown, of Kansas," continued Mr. S., with his voice pitched in the same high key, "I am sent here, sir, by the authorities in command, for to summon you to surrender; and, sir, I do it in the name of the Commonwealth of old Virginia—God bless her!"

"What terms do you offer?" inquired Brown.

"Terms!" exclaimed S. "I heard nothing said about them, sir, by those who sent me. What terms do you want?"

"I want to be allowed," said Brown, "to take my men and prisoners across the bridge to Maryland and as far up the river as the lock-house where I will release the prisoners unharmed, provided no pursuit shall be made until I get beyond that point."

The proposed terms were, of course, inadmissible; and after the paper containing them had been read by two or three of us it was handed to Lawson Botts, who threw it contemptuously upon the floor, and placing his foot on it, said: "Gentlemen, this is adding insult to injury. I think we ought to storm the engine-house, and take those fellows without further delay."

The Un-Civil War: Raiders and Outlaws in Missouri

When the South seceded (broke away) from the Union, that action divided states where citizens held opposing views of slavery. Missouri was one such divided state. Before the war, anti-slavery citizens' groups known as Jayhawkers or Redlegs raided farms, burning, looting, and freeing slaves. Meanwhile, pro-slavers, known as Bushwhackers, terrorized anti-slavery settlers.

The Missouri border during the Civil War was the scene of the greatest savagery in American history. William Quantrill, who led the pro-slavery violence, is considered by many historians to have been a psychopath who took advantage of the situation to satisfy his craving for violence.

As soon as the South seceded from the Union, as the citizens of Missouri were debating their loyalties, Northern soldiers entered the state and took possession of it. Many Missourians were not slave-holders and they had been sympathetic to the North, but the Union soldiers' heavy-handed tactics bred resentment. Those who sympathized with the South began a guerilla war, where neighbor fought against neighbor, and fighters

William Anderson—also known as Bloody Bill—was one of William Quantrill's followers. Together, the two men tortured and terrorized their way across Missouri, Kansas, and Texas.

often attacked without uniforms, making it difficult to judge between soldiers, raiders, and outlaws.

During the war, William Quantrill led many of the Confederate sympathizers, and his men were known as Quantrill's Raiders. Both sides fought out of uniform, burned homesteads, and killed civilians. The lawless and violent nature of these Civil War struggles carried over into the Wild West after the war, and the legendary James Gang, among other outlaw bands, was born from that conflict.

Snapshot from the Past

Reverend Beecher's Bibles: The Missouri Prairie, 1859

"Pa, there's a man here with a big box on his wagon, says it's for you," Jessica Parker called to her father.

Her father and brother stepped outside and gathered by the side of the buckboard. Now Jessica saw a word stamped on the side of the wooden crate: "Bibles." She scratched her head: what was Pa going to do with so many Bibles? But her father sure looked excited.

Rev. Henry Beecher was a well-known and controversial abolitionist during his day.

There'd been an awful lot of tension lately over the issue of slavery. Just last month, pro-slavery Bushwhackers had come by and threatened to run her family right off their land. Maybe someone back East thought there'd be less violence if all the Kansas folk read Scripture?

Pa and her brother grunted, lifting the box off the wagon. There was a metallic clanging noise as it hit the dirt. The driver pulled out a crowbar, and the men pried the top of the box open, and pulled out . . . rifles.

Jessica's eyes widened. The crate was filled with shiny new firearms.

The wagon driver explained. "Reverend Henry Beecher sent these to you folks. He supports the abolitionists in this territory, and while he prefers weapons of the Spirit, he knows some of you settlers require more . . . practical tools to defend yourselves." He nodded toward the guns. "He ships 'em labeled as Scripture, so the Bushwhackers won't capture the guns."

Jessica looked up at her father. He was not a violent man, but he was obviously pleased with the new gun in his hands. Jessica wasn't sure whether she was pleased or not.

Would it have been better, she wondered, if the case had been filled with real Bibles?

INCREDIBLE INDIVIDUAL
John Horse
(1812–1882)

John's mother was an escaped African slave, and his father was a Native Seminole tribesman: throughout his life, John strove for the rights of both Natives and Blacks—stances that sometimes put him outside United States law.

As a young man, John fought with the Seminole tribe against U.S. occupation of their lands. After this attempt failed, the government moved Horse to Oklahoma with other Seminoles, where he became a leader of transplanted tribal members. In 1844, the U.S. government decreed that people of African descent living among Native tribes could be captured and sold as slaves, so John moved his people into Mexico, where slavery had been abolished. After the Civil War, he worked for the U.S. Cavalry as a scout, but toward the end of his life he returned to Mexico to champion greater civil rights for Native people there.

EXTRA! EXTRA!

NATIONAL SENATOR BEATEN IN THE HOUSE CHAMBER

New York Tribune
May 23, 1856

By the news from Washington it will be seen that Senator Sumner has been savagely and brutally assaulted, while sitting in his seat in the Senate chamber, by the Hon. Mr. Brooks of South Carolina, the reason assigned therefore being that the Senator's remarks on Mr. Butler of South Carolina, who is uncle to the man who made the attack. The particulars show that Mr. Sumner was struck unawares over the head by a loaded cane and stunned, and then the ruffianly attack was continued with many blows, the Hon. Mr. Keitt of South Carolina keeping any of those around, who might be so disposed, from attempting a rescue... It is not in the least a cause for wonder that a member of the national House of Representatives, assisted by another as a fender-off, should attack a member of the national Senate.

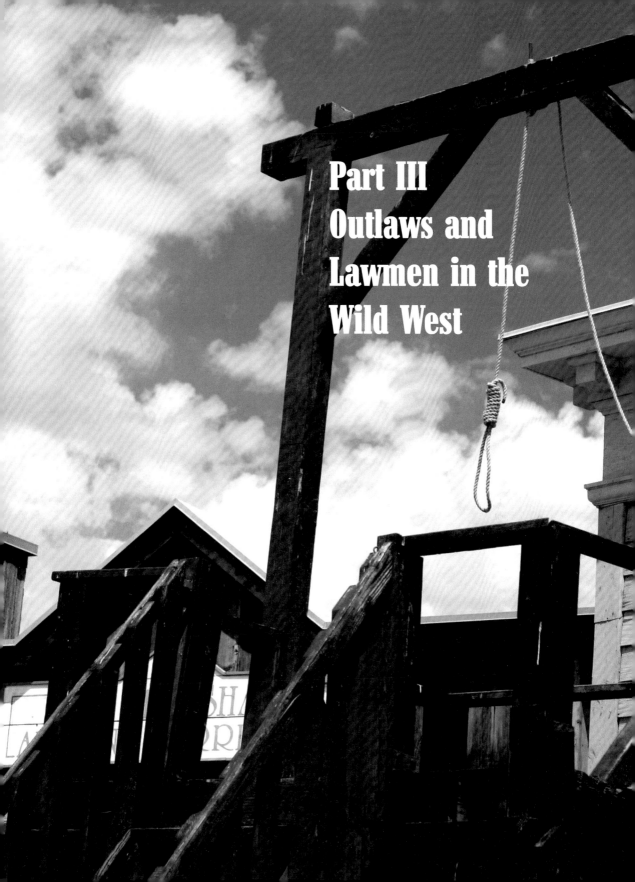

Part III
Outlaws and
Lawmen in the
Wild West

1867

1867 United States purchases Alaska from Russia.

1868

1868 The practice of "transportation" is officially ended —sending convicts from other countries to America as a form of punishment is no longer allowed.

1868 President Andrew Johnson is impeached under the charge of high crimes and misdemeanors.

1869

1869 Transcontinental Railroad completed on May 10.

1881

1881 Billy the Kid, or Henry McCarty, is killed on July 14 at 21 years old.

1882

1882 Jesse James, an outlaw, gang leader, and bank/train robber, dies.

1886

1886 The Statue of Liberty is dedicated on October 28.

1890

1890 Wounded Knee Massacre— Last battle in the American Indian Wars.

1870

1870 Fifteenth Amendment to the United States Constitution—Prohibits any citizen from being denied to vote based on their "race, color, or previous condition of servitude."

1870 Christmas is declared a national holiday.

1876

1876 Alexander Graham Bell invents the telephone.

1877

1877 Great Railroad Strike—Often considered the country's first nationwide labor strike.

1878

1878 Thomas Edison patents the phonograph on February 19.

1878 Thomas Edison invents the light bulb on October 22.

of the 1800s

1892

1892 Ellis Island is opened to receive immigrants coming into New York.

1896

1896 Plessy vs. Ferguson—Supreme Court case that rules that racial segregation is legal as long as accommodations are kept equal.

1896 Henry Ford builds his first combustion-powered vehicle, which he names the Ford Quadricycle.

1898

1898 The Spanish-American War—The United States gains control of Cuba, Puerto Rico, and the Philippines.

Gold and Vigilantes in California

In January 1848, John Sutter discovered gold at Coloma, California, and over the next couple years more than a quarter of a million fortune hunters headed west. The *New Yorker* magazine described the lawlessness of the gold fields in 1851:

> Miners were so greedy, treacherous and unreliable that no man's life was safe. Law and order were unknown; fights occurred daily, and anyone who could not protect himself with his fists was unfortunate. Every man carried a gun, all types of weapons that could shoot, cut, or stab—plain pocket pistols, Colt revolvers, and double-barreled guns. . . . Robbery and murder were commonplace, because men still preferred to steal gold dust rather than work for it and did not hesitate to take human lives if necessary.

The law was not quite "every man for himself"—but it was close to that. Miners formed vigilante bands (unofficial citizens' groups) to capture and hang the worst lawbreakers—at least they did so when they could pry themselves away from their diggings long enough to administer justice.

The Gold Rush also worsened Native-European relations in California. Mexican ranchers had once had a live-and-let-live approach to Native Californians. The miners, however, trespassed on Indian lands and killed Natives who stood between them and gold.

The gold miners' lust for gold drove the Native tribes of California to reservations, where they were forced to live in poverty.

EYEWITNESS ACCOUNT

Author James Penny Boyd wrote this account of the gold miners' wars with the Native tribes:

By 1853 the California tribes were pretty generally subdued and driven on to the five reservations set apart for them. These reservations were badly managed by the Government agents, who drew plentiful supplies from the Government but gave the Indians none. . . . Every Indian theft, every attempt on their part to scout and live, or to come back on their reservations to assert their rights, became a cause for war upon them, and it is quite probable that more perished in the difficulties which thus arose, than in all the prior effort to conquer them. Over 150 Indians were massacred by white settlers at Nome Cult in 1858, the only excuse being that they had driven off the cattle of the settlers from the reservation, because they were consuming the acorns on which the Indians depended for food. At King's River, the Indians were shot down by scores, and driven away because the Government would not support them and they had become a nuisance. In these humanitarian efforts to exterminate the natives, the settlers had the support of the state militia and there was no sentiment against this kind of murder. At Mattole Station and Humboldt Bay, similar massacres took place and there was no mercy shown to a refractory Indian. The next morning after the massacre at Humboldt Bay, sixty corpses of Indian men, women, boys and girls, showed how impious had been their refusal to go off to the then secluded region of Mendocino.

The character of the California settlers, gathered from all the ends of the earth, inspired by greed, with a golden stake in hand, was such as to make Indian wars of California frequent, short and decisive. They were wars which involved excessive cruelty, wars of extermination. The miners were a society by themselves, and a unit in their own protection. There was, of course, a powerful necessity for protection, as was shown not only in their wars with Indians, but in those stern measures which became the code of justice of their "Vigilance Committees." They were really at war with themselves, and peace and the reign of law came only after the rope had taught many of their own number, the same lessons their shotguns had impressed on the Indians.

Cattle, Sheep, Farms–and Violence

In Hollywood Western movies, good guys and bad guys draw guns from their holsters over issues of honor. In historical fact, greed motivated most of the shootings in the Old West, as competing factions defended their livelihoods at gunpoint. Typically, each side justified their actions as "justice" and cast parties that opposed them as "outlaws."

In Lincoln County, New Mexico, in 1878, rival ranches engaged in what historians call "The Lincoln County War." Billy the Kid, one of the most

legendary outlaws, served as hired hand for one of the ranches. Both sides claimed to be in the right with the law, and the two cattle companies killed nineteen men in their conflict.

Then sheepherders joined the picture: their flocks competed for grazing rights with the cattle, and sheep chewed the grass clear away, destroying the land's usefulness for cattlemen. As a result, cattle ranchers and sheep farmers fought bitter range wars.

Finally, the farmers staked out their claims, and protected their lands with barbed wire—hated by the old-style ranchers who were used to wide-open ranges for their cattle. Though the West seemed limitless, it quickly became clear that competing factions would have to settle their differences—by gun or by common agreement.

The Pinkerton Agency

The most efficient law enforcement in the post-Civil-War West was the Pinkerton Detective Agency. Allan Pinkerton migrated to the United States from Scotland in 1842, and then in

Billy the Kid died when he was only twenty-one, but his memory lives on. Some historians refer to him as the "Old West's favorite outlaw."

Allan Pinkerton's business flyer.

1850, established his private detective agency in Chicago. Its logo was an eye with the slogan "we never sleep"—hence detectives became known as "private eyes." Officers of the Agency were involved in operations against the James Gang, the Wild Bunch, and other famous Western outlaws.

The Legacy of War– the James Gang

As young men, Jesse and Frank James witnessed the brutalities of their divided state of Missouri. In 1863, an anti-slavery militia group tried to hang the boys' father, and they brutally whipped Jesse. The incident left scars in more ways than one: Jesse immediately joined Quantrill's Raiders and contributed his own share of violence to the bloody war.

After the war, the James brothers continued to live by the violent skills they had gained from the conflict, riding and shooting. They robbed banks and railroads. At the time, many citizens (especially Southerners) viewed these businesses as unjust and exploitive: the James Gang played up on public opinion, claiming to be "Robin Hood" types who stole to help the poor.

In 1882, Bob Ford, a member of the gang, shot Jesse in the back. He expected fame and gain for doing so, but instead received only hatred and scorn, so great was Jesse James' popularity.

Jesse James.

Snapshot from the Past

Sammy Saves the Farm

Oklahoma Territory, 1891 (Based on true events recorded in an old journal.)

"*Remember, stay clear of those ranchers, I know they want us off this land.*" Those were the parting words Sammy Houchen's husband gave her, just before he left to do business in the city.

For the next few days, the young wife enjoyed her solitude, and immersed herself in caring for the chickens, crops, and livestock, along with the other duties of their farm. Then, on the third night of solitude, a thunderstorm broke. Sammy huddled by the fire in their sod house, avoiding a few spots where water dripped steadily through the makeshift ceiling.

Then, between the sounds of thunder and rain, she heard another sound: a low vibration that seemed to come from the ground itself. She threw on a canvas poncho and grabbed the shotgun and a pouch full of shells her husband had left by the door.

Cattle herds were huge—and ranchers were often ruthless in their refusal to let grazing lands be turned into farms.

As she stepped out into the downpour, lightning flashed, illumining the plain to the east of their farm, and what she saw made Sammy catch her breath. A herd of cattle stampeded across the plain toward her farm. The ranchers were driving them toward the Houchens' land. The pounding hooves would destroy their crops, collapse their sod house, and—she realized with a flash of fright and anger—possibly take her life.

Another lightning flash: Sammy raised the double-barrel gun to her shoulder, leveled it, and pulled both triggers. It kicked hard, but it accomplished her purpose: a cow stumbled, then collapsed twenty paces ahead of her. The herd slowed.

Quickly, she shoved two more shells from the pouch into the chambers of the gun, took aim, fired again. Another cow came down. Sammy ran toward the fallen animals, to take shelter behind the bulwark of their bodies.

The herd began to move forward again, but they were divided now into two bellowing, pounding streams. One stream was heading past the Houchens' sod house, then past the chicken coop, but the stream of cattle on the left was still running toward their crop fields.

Sammy had just swung the gun to her left when she heard a snort just in front of her. Through the darkness and rain, she saw a bull's enormous horns just yards away. She barely had time to point the gun at its forehead and pull. The remaining barrel discharged, and the bull collapsed at her feet.

With shaking hands, she reloaded both barrels again and fired two shots off to her left. Two more steers down, and now she had formed a sizable wall of dead cattle. The stampeding herd, still moving forward, parted in two directions and thundered past her farm, leaving it intact.

Sammy collapsed into the mud, soaked through, gasping for breath. She had never dreamed that she was capable of such actions as this night's work. Truly, her new life in the West had made her a new kind of woman.

Natives Fight for Their Homelands

European settlers rolled across the West like waves of the ocean, wagon train after wagon train—and the First Nations people who had lived in these lands for thousands of years strove to preserve their way of life. Between 1851 and 1871, the U.S. government forced the nations of the Oceti Sakowin Confederation—now usually called Sioux—onto increasingly smaller land holdings, where government agents pressured them to adopt European

The courage and determination of Chief Dull Knife (also called Morning Star) was in large part the reason why the Northern Cheyenne still possess a homeland in their traditional country (present-day Montana).

This photograph shows the U.S. forces standing beside the mass grave of the people they had slaughtered at Wounded Knee. Eighty-four men, forty-four women, and eighteen children were killed.

ways. Then, in 1871, trespassing miners discovered gold in the Black Hills, and the U.S. government took over this sacred land, an area known to the

Native people as "the heart of everything that is." Conflicts ensued, including the Sioux victory at the Battle of Little Bighorn, and, later, the terrible massacre of Native Americans at Wounded Knee.

After Little Big Horn, the government forced the Northern Cheyenne Tribe, who had fought alongside the Oceti Sakowin, to relocate to Oklahoma, where many of them died from hunger and disease. In 1878, Chief Dull Knife announced to the government agent in Oklahoma, "I am going north to my own country. I do not want to see blood spilt about this agency. Let me get a little distance away. Then if you want to fight, I will fight you, and we can make bloody ground at that place." Miraculously, a small number of the Northern Cheyenne outwitted and outmaneuvered thousands of government troops, relocating in their ancestral lands where they still live today.

Barboncito is credited with being a "peace chief" who laid the foundation for the long-term survival of his people's culture.

Further west, the Diné people (Navajo) fought against Kit Carson and U.S. soldiers, who waged a war of extermination against them. Survivors were rounded up and taken to Fort Sumner. Gus Bighorse recalled the move: "The trip is on foot. People are shot on the spot if they say they are tired or sick or if they stop to help someone. If a woman is in labor with a baby, she is killed." Conditions at the fort were little better. Diné chief Barboncito pled with General Sherman to let his people return to their own lands, in order to ensure their survival. His request was granted; and the people trekked by foot back to their homeland. When sacred Mount Taylor came into view, they sat down and cried from happiness and relief.

Reservation land looking toward Mount Taylor.

Card Sharks and Soiled Doves

In the cattle towns and railroad and mining camps, gambling was the most popular form of entertainment. Claims of cheating (whether real or imagined) and testy tempers were a common risk at the card table, so gamblers typically carried tiny concealed pistols known as Derringers or small knives concealed in the palm of the hand, both useful for sudden self-defense.

Prostitution provided a way for destitute women to survive, and west of the Mississippi, most of the "soiled doves" (as these women were known) were recent immigrants, from China or Europe—women whose limited language and career skills doomed their chances of survival in the West. Though glamorized by Hollywood, the life of an Old West prostitute was cruel and short. Like the card sharks, they defended themselves with small, concealed arms.

Gamblers and prostitutes were not technically "outlaws," as both professions were legal in the Western Territories for several decades after the Civil War. (Mormon communities were the exception to this.) However, while these trades were within the law, drunkenness, greed, and cheating often created violent situations where survival depended on first shooting—and then fleeing.

In this Old West town, the gallows stood next to the saloon, where it would be handy for dealing with the violence and crime that often occurred inside the building.

Chinese laborers helped build the railroad tracks across the nation, but they often faced violence and prejudice.

Railroad Hell Camps

Railroad lines, linking sides of the country together, were the greatest civilizing influence on the frontier—after they were completed. However, while companies laid the railroad lines, they created makeshift towns (actually just sprawling camps), the most violent and lawless parts of the West during their brief existence. Chinese and Irish workers labored under unsafe conditions for minimal pay; drinking, gambling, and whoring were common amusements, and often, there was no law in these temporary communities.

Canyon Diablo, Arizona, began in 1880 when railroad construction slowed down to bridge the canyon. The makeshift town quickly became known as "the toughest Hellhole in the West." The town lasted only fourteen months, but during that time it boasted seven marshals, one of whom served for only five hours before someone gunned him down. While sheriffs came and went, violence raged on in the railroad town—resulting in more than 2,000 deaths in slightly more than a year's time.

Gunfights in the Streets

The legendary Wild West was built on the idea of the Colt six-shot revolver and the "fast draw" gunman. Samuel Colt's Patented Revolving Pistol was called "the great equalizer," the firearm most prized by all who could attain one. Between 1866 and 1900, more than 20,000 men died from gunfire west of the Mississippi; it was truly the age of the gunfighter.

A man's ability to pull his gun faster than his opponent meant he would live to fight again.

Wild Bill Hickok

"Wild Bill" Hickok was the first man to gain fame as a fast-draw gunslinger. Eastern novelists portrayed Hickok as one of the good guys—and Hickok himself claimed he "never killed a man except in self defense or official duty"—but in fact he led a checkered career as scout, sheriff, and gambler. Hickok died on August 2, 1876, in Deadwood, shot in the back while playing poker.

INCREDIBLE INDIVIDUAL
Orrin Porter Rockwell

Although he is little known today, Orrin Porter Rockwell was, in his time, as famous as any Western legend. A Mormon (Latter Day Saint), he served as bodyguard for the prophet and founder of that movement—Joseph Smith—and for Smith's successor Brigham Young. Joseph Smith once declared: "I prophesy, in the name of the Lord, that you—Orrin Porter Rockwell—so long as ye shall remain loyal and true to thy faith, need fear no enemy. Cut not thy hair and no bullet or blade can harm thee." The prophecy seemed to come true: over the following decades Rockwell was involved in as many violent altercations as any of his gun-slinging contemporaries, serving as a scout, bodyguard, and United States Marshal—yet he was never even touched by any opponent.

Cool under fire, and unerringly deadly with his guns, people called Rockwell the "Avenging Angel." Historians attribute more than forty deaths to him, so Rockwell probably killed more men than any other Western gunfighter. Nonetheless, Rockwell claimed "I never killed anyone that didn't need killing."

EXTRA! EXTRA!

GUNFIGHT AT THE OK CORRAL

Tombstone Daily Epitaph,
October 27, 1881

Wyatt Earp

Mr. Coleman says: I was in the O.K. Corral at 2:30 p.m., when I saw the two Clantons and the two McLowrys in an earnest conversation across the street in Dunbar's corral. I went up the street and notified Sheriff Behan and told him it was my opinion they meant trouble, and it was his duty, as sheriff, to go and disarm them. I told him they had gone to the West End Corral. I then went and saw Marshal Virgil Earp and notified him to the same effect. I then met Billy Allen and we walked through the O.K. Corral, about fifty yards behind the sheriff.

On reaching Fremont Street I saw Virgil Earp, Wyatt Earp, Morgan Earp and Doc Holliday, in the center of the street, all armed. I had reached Bauer's meat market. Johnny Behan had just left the cowboys, after having a conversation with them. I went along to Fly's photograph gallery, when I heard Virg Earp say, "Give up your arms or throw up your arms." There was some reply made by Frank McLowry, when firing became general, over thirty shots being fired. Tom McLowry fell first, but raised and fired again before he died. Bill Clanton fell next, and raised to fire again when Mr. Fly took his revolver from him. Frank McLowry ran a few rods and fell. Morgan Earp was shot through and fell. Doc Holliday was hit in the left hip but kept on firing. Virgil Earp was hit in the third or fourth fire, in the leg which staggered him but he kept up his effective work. Wyatt Earp stood up and fired in rapid succession, as cool as a cucumber, and was not hit. Doc Holliday was as calm as though at target practice and fired rapidly. After the firing was over, Sheriff Behan went up to Wyatt Earp and said, "I'll have to arrest you." Wyatt replied: "I won't be arrested today. I am right here and am not going away. You have deceived me. You told me these men were disarmed; I went to disarm them."

INCREDIBLE INDIVIDUAL
"Doc" Holliday

John Henry Holliday (1852–1887) was a dentist and gambler who frequented the cattle and mining towns of the Wild West. When Doc was twenty-one, a doctor diagnosed him with tuberculosis and told him that he would live but a few months if he stayed in his native state of Georgia—so Doc headed west. Because of his coughing, few people trusted his dental skills, so Doc took up gambling instead. Living by the cards, Doc sometimes relied on deception and was involved in a number of deadly altercations. Though his reputation was unsavory, Doc was close friends with Wyatt Earp, and he stood and fought beside the Earp brothers at the famous Gunfight at the OK Corral.

Historians have remembered Doc as both a hero and a villain; he showed marks of deep loyalty for his friends and cold callousness toward his enemies, and he employed his skill in whichever direction paid best. In these respects, he was like many of his peers in the violent Wild West.

Someone once asked Doc if his conscience bothered him over the men he had gunned down; he replied, "No, I coughed that up with my lungs long ago."

Justice Comes to the West

By the 1880s, rule-of-law became more common in the West. The rapidly growing towns from Kansas to California realized that their future prosperity depended on a lessening of vice, so communities turned to hiring peace officers to enforce justice. At the same time, there was still enough violence that any peace officer had to be willing to face down his opponent and shoot to kill when necessary. It wasn't easy to get "squeaky clean" gunmen, so, to quote Western historian R.L. Wilson, "the line separating lawman from criminal was sometimes faint."

Virgil Earp (Wyatt's brother) was City Marshall in Tombstone, Arizona, in 1881, when a group of cowboys came into town defying the "no guns in town" ordinance. The miscreants were members of the Clanton and McLaury families, who had previously engaged in verbal threats against the Earp brothers. The Earps and Clantons stood on opposite sides of political and economic factions in the town.

A modern-day reenactment of the gunfight at the OK Corral in Tombstone.

The town of Tombstone, Arizona, saw more than its share of violence—but law and order finally prevailed.

Virgil quickly appointed his brothers Wyatt and Morgan and their friend Doc Holliday as assistant marshals, and they walked over to the OK Corral where their opponents waited. Minutes later, the McLaurys and Billy Clanton were mortally wounded, and Virgil and Morgan Earp were injured, but the Earp faction had clearly gotten the upper hand. Tombstone's two newspapers disagreed on the justice of the gunfight, reflecting the town's divided loyalties between the dueling parties.

For the next several years, there were a series of reprisal killings between the two groups, with Wyatt Earp and friends prevailing. This battle for control of Southern Arizona was typical of the way justice came to the West: bloody, controversial, but tending toward enforcement of the law in the long run.

EXTRA! EXTRA!

A HANGING

The New Mexican,
December 15, 1875

Before mounting the platform, the condemned man, Mr. Wilson, shook hands with several whom he recognized, and mounted the scaffold calm and collected. The escort was drawn in line fronting the gallows, whilst four men dismounted and kept back the crowd, which by this time had increased considerably.

Whilst on the scaffold the death warrant was read first in English and then in Spanish, after which the dying declaration written and signed by Wilson was read and translated. He then received the extreme unction and the merciful sheriff declared that the execution would be stayed for half an hour. However, the leading men of the town, actuated by pity for the poor unfortunate, entered such a vigorous protest against such barbarous proceedings that the sheriff went ahead with the execution.

The priest descended from the scaffold, the black cap was adjusted, and the prisoner, with hands tied behind and the noose around his neck, awaited his doom.

The sheriff descended from the scaffold, and in an instant justice, so long outraged, was avenged, and the perpetrator of one of the foulest murders which ever disgraced a civilized community was no more.

After hanging nine and a half minutes, the body was cut down and placed in the coffin, when it was discovered that life was not yet extinct. A rope was fastened around his neck, and the crowd drew the inanimate body from the coffin and suspended it from the gallows where it hanged for twenty minutes longer. It was then cut down and placed in the coffin and buried.

Outlaws Fade into the Sunset

Led by dapper Butch Cassidy, the Wild Bunch rustled cattle, held-up banks, and robbed trains throughout the west in the final years of the 1800s. At the turn of the century, they held up the Great Northern Express train near Wagner, Montana, where they looted $40,000.00. Pursued by Pinkerton detectives, the gang split up. The most famous members—Butch and the Sundance Kid—fled to South America, where they faded into history.

The Wild Bunch; Butch Cassidy is seated at the right.

With the demise of the Wild Bunch, the historical era of the Wild West came to an end. Shortly after that, the new technology of motion-picture filmmaking began to immortalize the gunslingers. Wyatt Earp and a few others lived to bridge the gap between the West of Hollywood and that of history.

At the same time that Hollywood immortalized the violence of the 1800s, a new breed of criminal rose up. They replaced the six-shooter with automatic weapons and turned big-city streets once again into centers of violence. First alcohol (during Prohibition), then illegal drugs fueled criminal activities. Gangs and drug wars continue to claim lives today.

Judges like Roy Bean dispensed justice and gradually tamed the Wild West.

Think About It

Americans continue to be fascinated by the "gunslingers" of the West and the lawmen who fought to bring them to justice. Even in the twenty-first century, shootouts, stagecoach robberies and outlaw gangs on horseback are material for books, TV shows, and movies.

- What is it about the outlaws of 1800s America that has made them so legendary?

- Are the men who brought law and order to the West as famous as the "bad guys"? What does that tell you?

- Justice on the frontier was often very different than justice today. What dangers were there in the actions of keepers of the peace back then? In what ways is the modern system of law enforcement and the courts better? Are there some ways it isn't as good?

Words Used in This Book

abolitionists: Those people, before the Civil War, who wanted slavery to be outlawed.

activists: People who argue and protest strongly for or against a certain issue.

altercations: Loud and angry disagreements or arguments.

barbarous: Cruel and harsh.

benevolent: Kind and compassionate; wishing to do good.

callousness: Emotional hardness; lack of sympathy or compassion.

card sharks: Expert card players who use skill, and sometimes cheating, to win, mainly at poker.

civil rights: The rights people have because they are citizens.

controversial: Something that people often disagree about.

demise: Death or end of existence.

destitute: Extremely poor; lacking an income or other way to get food, clothes, and shelter.

economic: Having to do with money and its production, distribution, and use.

exploitive: Being used selfishly and unethically.

extortion: Using power or position to get money, goods, or privileges.

expunged: Gotten rid of; wiped out.

factions: Groups within a larger group or organization, usually disagreeing or competing with each other.

fetid: Stinking; having a bad smell.

First Nations: Another term for Native Americans.

glamorized: Portrayed in a way that makes something look more beautiful, exciting, or romantic than it actually is.

guerilla: Related to fighting by underground or informal troops, usually using tactics such as surprise attacks or sabotage, for example.

immortalized: Made famous, so that a person or thing will be remembered forever.

intemperate: Unrestrained, uncontrolled; drinking excessive amounts of alcohol.

lynching: Punishing a person without legal authority, usually carried out by a mob, and usually by hanging.

militia: A group of citizen soldiers, as opposed to those enlisted in the military.

miscreants: Wrongdoers; evil people.

nullity: Something without value or legal power.

ordinance: A decree or law.

peers: People of equal position or status to another person.

pestiferous: Dirty, infected, causing disease.

pilfering: Stealing, especially in small amounts.

popular vote: A vote taken by individual voters on a candidate or issue, as opposed to a vote taken by elected representatives.

precedent: A case or situation that acts as a guide for situations that happen later.

profligacy: Lack of self-restraint; recklessness; excessive and shameful pursuit of pleasure.

ruffian: A thug; a tough, rowdy person.

rustlers: People who steal cattle or other livestock from a farm or ranch.

seceded: Formally separated or broke away from an organization or political body.

vigilantes: People who take the law into their own hands and do not go through official and legal methods.

Find Out More

In Books

Krohn, Katherine E. *Wild West Women*. Minneapolis, Minn.: Lerner, 2005.

Olson, Tod. *How to Get Rich in the California Gold Rush: An Adventurer's Guide to the Fabulous Riches Discovered in 1848*. Des Moines, Iowa: National Geographic Children's Books, 2008.

Sheinkin, Steve. *Which Way to the Wild West?: Everything Your Schoolbooks Didn't Tell You About Westward Expansion*. New York: Roaring Brook Press, 2008.

Stefoff, Rebecca. *American Voices from the Wild West*. New York: Benchmark Books, 2006.

Swanson, Wayne. *Why the West Was Wild*. Toronto, Canada: Annick Press, 2004.

Woog, Adam. *Jesse James*. New York: Chelsea House, 2010.

Woog, Adam. *Wyatt Earp*. New York: Chelsea House, 2010.

On the Internet

American Experience: Transcontinental Railroad
www.pbs.org/wgbh/amex/tcrr

American West: A Celebration of the Human Spirit
www.americanwest.com

Legends of America: Old West Legends
www.legendsofamerica.com/we-oldwestpeople.html

The Wild West
www.thewildwest.org

Wild West, History Net
www.historynet.com/magazines/wild_west

Wyatt Earp History Page
www.wyattearp.net

The websites listed on this page were active at the time of publication. The publisher is not responsible for websites that have changed their address or discontinued operation since the date of publication. The publisher will review and update the websites upon each reprint.

Index

Picture Credits

About the Author and the Consultant

Kenneth McIntosh is the author of more than sixty books, including titles in the Mason Crest series North American Indians Today. He also teaches college classes. He and his wife live in Flagstaff, Arizona, a town with an abundance of heritage sites from the 1800s.

John Gillis is a Rutgers University Professor of History Emeritus. A graduate of Amherst College and Stanford University, he has taught at Stanford, Princeton, University of California at Berkeley, as well as Rutgers. Gillis is well known for his work in social history, including pioneering studies of age relations, marriage, and family. The author or editor of ten books, he has also been a fellow at both St. Antony's College, Oxford, and Clare Hall, Cambridge.